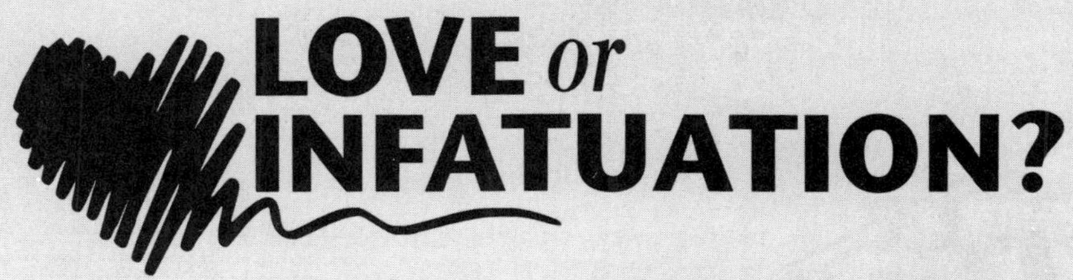

A 4-week course to help junior highers explore the complexities of dating relationships from a Christian perspective

by Amy Nappa

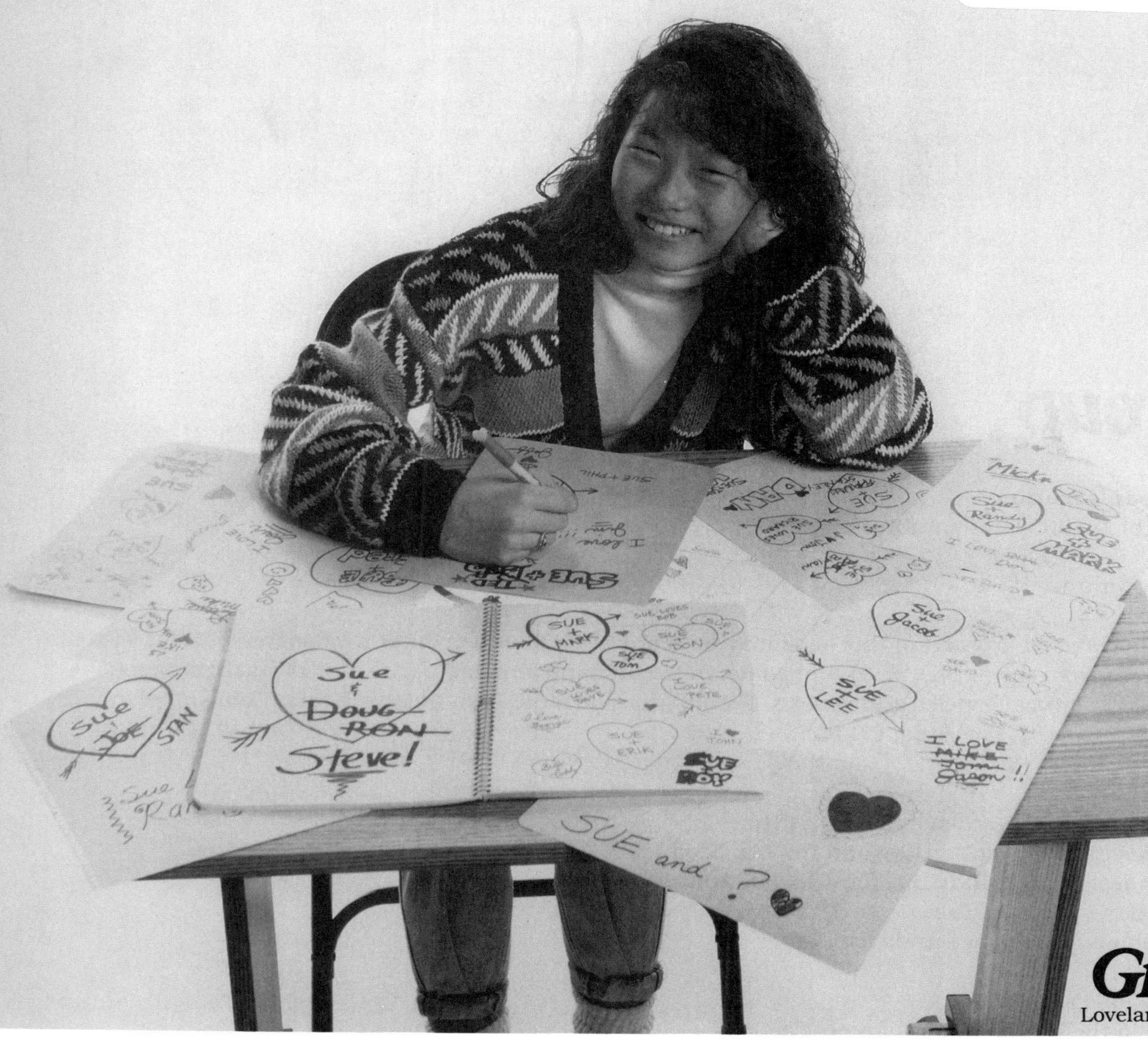

Group®
Loveland, Colorado

Group®

Love or Infatuation?

Second Printing, 1994

Credits
Edited by Michael Warden and Lois Keffer
Cover designed by Jill Nordbye and DeWain Stoll
Interior designed by Judy Bienick and Jan Aufdemberge
Illustrations by Doug Hall
Cover photo by Brenda Rundback

ISBN 1-55945-128-9
Printed in the United States of America.

CONTENTS

INTRODUCTION

LOVE OR INFATUATION?

"Trevor broke up with me yesterday," Halley confided in her friend, Kimber. "He's such a slime. I hate him."

"What's his problem?" Kimber asked.

"He wanted to, well, you know, go all the way."

"Well, how long were you going out?"

"A week and five days," Halley answered. It was one of her longer relationships.

• • •

Such is love in the life of a junior higher. Crushes come and go; sex is debated; hearts are broken; then it's off to a new romance.

But sometimes what kids feel seems more serious than a passing crush, and not all teenagers say no to sex.

Most middle schoolers feel uncomfortable talking with their parents about sex, and the reverse is also true. With everyone waiting for someone else to cover the topic, kids are looking to their peers and the media for guidance. The information they get from these sources is distorted: Sex and love are interchangeable, and neither requires a commitment.

As students move into the junior high years, friendships with members of the opposite sex are more acceptable. While most parents would probably like their kids to wait until they are 16, many young people begin dating around 14. To the junior higher, it suddenly seems like everyone is "going out." Going out can simply mean identifying with one special person of the opposite sex, being seen

Broken Dreams

- 4 percent of 12-year-olds have already had sexual intercourse.
- 10 percent of 13-year-olds have experimented with sex.
- 20 percent of 14-year-olds have had sex.

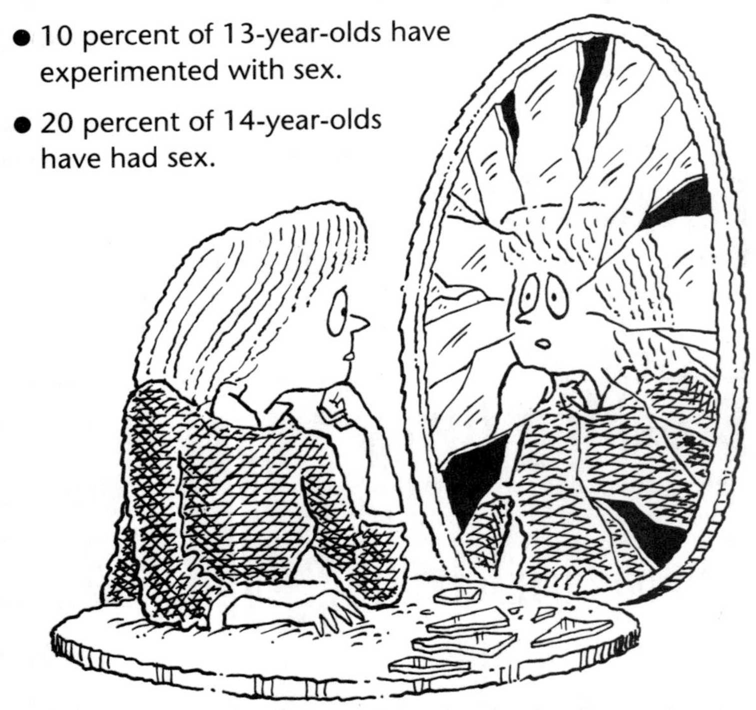

with that person at school events and sharing long and frequent phone conversations. Group dates—with several friends getting together for special activities—are also a common practice.

Junior highers need a strong Christian perspective as they begin this new phase of life. They need to know the difference between true love and infatuation. How do healthy relationships with the opposite sex begin? Or end? And what about sex?

Of course, junior highers have their own ideas about all of these questions. Unfortunately, many of these ideas are misguided and incorrect. This course helps students define true love and consider how it applies to various aspects of their relationships with the opposite sex.

The Halleys, Kimbers, and Trevors in your junior high groups are making choices about sex, love and infatuation that could change their lives. You can help them made the right choices.

COURSE OBJECTIVES

By the end of this course, your students will:

- determine the differences between love and infatuation;
- distinguish realistic qualities they should look for in members of the opposite sex;
- explore ways to improve communication with the opposite sex;
- discover positive ways to end a relationship; and
- realize that love involves treating others better than ourselves.

HOW TO USE THIS COURSE

ACTIVE LEARNING

Think back on an important lesson you've learned in life. Did you learn it from reading about it? from hearing about it? from something you experienced? Chances are, the most important lessons you've learned came from something you've experienced. That's what active learning is— learning by doing. And active learning is a key element in Group's Active Bible Curriculum.

Active learning leads students in doing things that help them understand important principles, messages and ideas. It's a discovery process that helps kids internalize what they learn.

Each lesson section in Group's Active Bible Curriculum plays an important part in active learning:

The **Opener** involves kids in the topic in fun and unusual ways.

The **Action and Reflection** includes an experience designed to evoke specific feelings in the students. This section also processes those feelings through "How did you feel?" questions and applies the message to situations kids face.

The **Bible Application** actively connects the topic with the Bible. It helps kids see how the Bible is relevant to the situations they face.

The **Commitment** helps students internalize the Bible's message and commit to make changes in their lives.

The **Closing** funnels the lesson's message into a time of creative reflection and prayer.

When you put all the sections together, you get a lesson that's fun to teach. And kids get messages they'll remember.

BEFORE THE 4-WEEK SESSION

- Read the Introduction, the Course Objectives and This Course at a Glance.
- Decide how you'll publicize the course using the clip art on the Publicity Page (p. 9). Prepare fliers, newsletter articles and posters as needed.
- Look at the Bonus Ideas (p. 43) and decide which ones you'll use.

BEFORE EACH LESSON

- Read the opening statements, Objectives and Bible Basis for the lesson. The Bible Basis shows how specific passages relate to junior highers and middle schoolers today.
- Choose which Opener and Closing options to use. Each is appropriate for a different kind of group.
- Gather necessary supplies from This Lesson at a Glance.
- Read each section of the lesson. Adjust where necessary for your class size and meeting room.

HELPFUL HINTS

- The approximate minutes listed give you an idea of how long each activity will take. Each lesson is designed to take 35 to 60 minutes. Shorten or lengthen activities as needed to fit your group.
- If you see you're going to have extra time, do an activity or two from the "If You Still Have Time . . . " box or from the Bonus Ideas (p. 43).
- Dive into the activities with the kids. Don't be a spectator. The lesson will be more successful and rewarding to both you and your students.
- Though some kids may at first think certain activities are "silly," they'll enjoy them and they'll remember the messages from these activities long after the lesson is over. As one Active Bible Curriculum user has said, "I can ask the kids questions about a lesson I did three weeks ago and they actually remember what I taught!" And that's the whole idea of teaching . . . isn't it?

Have fun with the activities you lead. Remember, it is Jesus who encourages us to become "like little children." Besides, how often do your kids get *permission* to express their childlike qualities?

- The answers given after discussion questions are responses your students *might* give. They aren't the only answers or the "right" answers. If needed, use them to spark discussion. Kids won't always say what you wish they'd say. That's why some of the responses given are negative or controversial. If someone responds negatively, don't be shocked. Accept the person and use the opportunity to explore other angles of the issue.

THIS COURSE AT A GLANCE

Before you dive into the lessons, familiarize yourself with each lesson aim. Then read the scripture passages.

- Study them as a background to the lessons.
- Use them as a basis for your personal devotion.
- Think about how they relate to kids' circumstances today.

LESSON 1: INFATUATION SENSATION

Lesson Aim: To help junior highers understand the difference between having a crush on someone and being in love.

Bible Basis: I Corinthians 13:4-8a.

LESSON 2: SEX IS NOT LOVE

Lesson Aim: To help junior highers examine how sex should fit into the overall scheme of relationships.

Bible Basis: Ruth 2:8-9, 13-16 and 2 Samuel 11:2-5.

LESSON 3: FRIENDS FIRST

Lesson Aim: To help junior highers discover that friendship is the foundation of all healthy relationships.

Bible Basis: Philippians 2:3-8.

LESSON 4: BREAKING AWAY

Lesson Aim: To help junior highers learn how to handle relationships when they end.

Bible Basis: Luke 6:27-28, 31 and Galatians 5:15.

PUBLICITY PAGE

Grab your junior highers' attention! Photocopy this page, and then cut and paste the clip art of your choice in your church bulletin or newsletter to advertise this course on love and infatuation. Or photocopy and use the ready-made flier as a bulletin insert. Permission to photocopy clip art is granted for local church use.

Splash the clip art on posters, fliers or even postcards! Just add the vital details: the date and time the course begins and where you'll meet.

It's that simple.

LOVE or
INFATUATION?

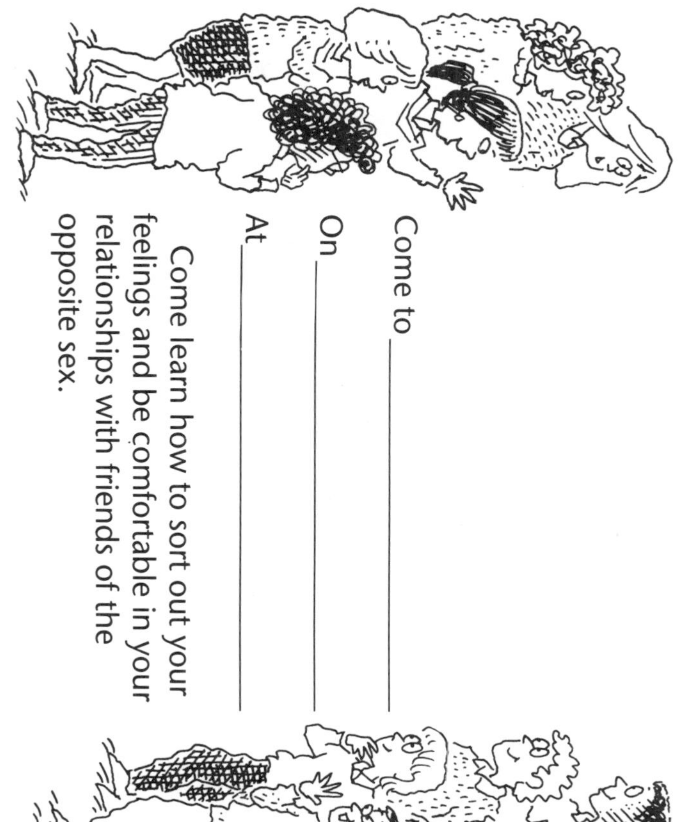

INFATUATION SENSATION

LESSON 1

In fairy tales and movies it's love at first sight, a quick romance, then off to living happily ever after. Unfortunately, things don't always work that way in real life.

Junior highers get mixed messages about the nature of love and infatuation. We can show our kids that infatuation is normal, but that it doesn't always lead to love—or even to a date!

LESSON AIM

To help junior highers understand the difference between having a crush on someone and being in love.

OBJECTIVES

Students will:

- **see how their choices affect their future and their relationships;**
- **decide the actions of fictional characters who are in love or who have a crush on someone;**
- **act out a fairy tale that turns into a real-life disaster; and**
- **create a "wanted" poster describing a "perfect" (but realistic) date.**

BIBLE BASIS

1 CORINTHIANS 13:4-8a

Look up the following scripture. Then read the background paragraphs to see how the passage relates to your junior highers and middle schoolers.

In **1 Corinthians 13:4-8a**, Paul gives a brief overview of what true love is.

"Love never ends" is a tough order to fill. But God's word defines this perfect kind of love through specific actions.

Junior highers can understand that love isn't a mushy feeling that turns your stomach into butterflies whenever "The One" brushes against your arm. Through this passage, kids can see what love is by learning how to express it—and how *not* to express it.

THIS LESSON AT A GLANCE

Section	Minutes	What Students Will Do	Supplies
Opener (Option 1)	5 to 10	**Take Your Pick**—Vote on listed options to choose which is best.	Newsprint, tape, marker
(Option 2)		**Now . . . and Later**—Make choices about what they want to collect.	Cloth strips, small candies, forks, a cake, plates
Action and Reflection	15 to 20	**Cinderdude**—Act out a skit about romance.	"Cinderdude" handout (p. 18)
Bible Application	10 to 15	**What's Love Got to Do With It?**—Choose appropriate actions for fictional characters.	Bibles
Commitment	5 to 10	**Wanted—The Ideal Date**—Make "Wanted" posters showing qualities desired in relationships.	Paper, markers
Closing (Option 1)	up to 5	**Crush**—Celebrate by drinking Crush soft drinks.	Crush soft drinks
(Option 2)		**Love Me or Leave Me**—Share a quality that makes class members worthy of more than a crush.	

The Lesson

OPENER
(5 to 10 minutes)

☐ OPTION 1: TAKE YOUR PICK

Read the listed options below one at a time and instruct kids to vote on which is best. If there is a tie, you cast the deciding vote. Write kids' choices on newsprint.

Which is best?

- green beans or french fries
- a brown Volvo or a red Jaguar
- a hot fudge sundae or an apple
- new Nike athletic shoes or sneakers from Kmart
- watching television or washing the car
- hanging out at the mall or helping your brother with homework
- wearing new clothes or wearing hand-me-downs from your cousin
- walking or taking the bus

Ask:

● Were these easy or hard for you to choose between? Explain.

● Imagine yourself 10 or 20 years from now—if you end up having a heart attack or in debt from overspending, will you wish you'd made different choices? Why or why not?

Say: **Sometimes we pick what seems good at the moment, but later we wish we'd been more careful in our selection. This lesson will help us look more closely at our choices in dealing with dating, love and sex.**

☐ OPTION 2: NOW . . . AND LATER

Before the lesson, hide a cake somewhere in the room where kids won't see it. Or put it in your church kitchen until you need it in the lesson.

Form groups of three or four. Have group members stand side by side and tie their wrists together with cloth strips. At one end of the room, place a supply of small wrapped candies. At the other end of the room, place a supply of plastic forks. Have all the groups stand in the middle of the room.

Say: **When I say "go," you and your group members may head for either end of the room to pick up as much candy as you can or to pick up a couple of forks. You may only go to one side of the room, and you may not change your mind once you've left the middle of the room. Ready . . . Go!**

After groups have cleaned out your candy or picked up the forks, ask:

● How easy was the decision you had to make? (It wasn't easy, I wanted to know what the fork was for; it was easy, I wanted the candy.)

● How is that like the way you make choices in relationships? (I don't always know what to do; I sometimes wonder if what looks good today is the best choice.)

● How did the choice you wanted affect your relationship with the rest of your group? (They didn't like me; they wanted to do something different so we didn't get along.)

Bring out the cake and serve it on paper plates to the people who chose the forks (if any). If no one picked the forks, show kids the cake and tell them what would've happened had they picked the forks.

Ask:

● How do you feel now about the decision your group made? (Bad, I wanted the cake; good, we chose the best thing.)

● How did your choice affect the future outcome of this activity? (If we thought ahead, we made a good decision on what to pick up; we wanted the candy now, so we didn't care about the future.)

Say: **As in this activity, our choices in life affect our relationships. And they can have an impact on our future options too. Today, we'll explore some of the differences**

between love and infatuation and how the choices we make in relationships can affect our future.

ACTION AND REFLECTION
(15 to 20 minutes)

CINDERDUDE

Ask for several volunteers to act out the "Cinderdude" story (p. 18)—a funny version of "Cinderella." Give the volunteers photocopies of the script and send them into another room to practice for a few minutes.

While the actors are out of the room, tell the rest of the group members that they have a role in the skit as well—as disrupters.

Have a couple of guys agree to "fight" in the back of the room when they get a cue from you. At the same time, have a few volunteers throw paper wads onto the stage area. Don't allow any negative comments, but have the group act disruptive and uninterested in the skit.

Call the actors back in and begin the skit. When they are about half-way through, give the cue for the "disrupters" to begin fighting and throwing paper wads. After a minute or so, stop the skit and call everyone together.

Ask:

- **Those of you in the skit, how did you feel when your fairy tale was interrupted?** (Frustrated; hurt.)
- **Those of you who were in the audience, how did you feel about ruining their skit?** (I enjoyed it; it would have been more fun to see the end of the skit.)
- **How is this experience similar to having a crush on someone?** (You expect a fairy-tale ending, but it doesn't usually happen; it can be a disaster.)
- **When you have a crush on someone, how do you feel?** (Nervous; excited.)
- **Is a crush or infatuation the same thing as love? Why or why not?** (Yes, it's the first stage of love; no, infatuation is immature and not based in reality.)

Say: **Sometimes we want our love lives to be like fairy tales. We meet someone—or maybe only see them on television or in a picture. We dream of getting to know that person, falling in love, maybe even getting married. But in real life things rarely turn out that way. For some reason our infatuation ends and we move on to a new crush. It seems we weren't really in love after all. Let's see if we can learn more about the difference between infatuation and real love.**

BIBLE APPLICATION
(10 to 15 minutes)

WHAT'S LOVE GOT TO DO WITH IT?

Ask a student to read aloud 1 Corinthians 13:4-8a.

Say: **I am going to read aloud a situation to you; then I want you all to decide what the best action would be and what part of this passage supports your answer.**

Situation 1: **Jason asks Penny to go to the mall. When**

they get there, Penny sees her cousin and they stand there talking for 20 minutes. She never even introduces Jason.

Ask:

- **If Jason loves Penny what would he do?** (Be patient, even if he is bored—love is patient.)
- **If Jason just had a crush on Penny, what might he do?** (Get mad and leave; try to go on a date with Penny's cousin.)

Situation 2: **Manuel asks Sasha to go to the movies with him. While they are waiting for the movie to start, Manuel's old girlfriend, Jill, walks in. Manuel asks Jill to sit with him and Sasha. She accepts.**

Ask:

- **If Sasha just has a crush on Manuel, what might she do?** (Yell at him; be rude to Jill.)
- **If Sasha loves Manuel, what will she do?** (Be polite to Jill—love is kind, it is not rude, it is not easily angered; not act jealous—love does not envy.)

Situation 3: **Mandy and Tony have a class together and Mandy thinks Tony is the cutest guy she's ever seen. When Tony asks Mandy to go to the movies with him, she's thrilled and tells all her friends. But when Tony comes to her house to pick her up, Mandy is dismayed to see that Tony has a huge zit on the top of his nose.**

Ask:

- **If Mandy loves Tony, what would she do?** (Go to the movie anyway and ignore Tony's imperfection—love patiently accepts all things.)
- **If Mandy only has a crush on Tony, what might she do?** (Make an excuse not to go; go with him but wear dark glasses.)

Situation Four: **Tressa and Randy have been dating each other for about three months when Randy starts putting pressure on Tressa to have sex with him. Tressa says no.**

Ask:

- **If Randy only has a crush on Tressa, what might he do?** (Stop dating her; spread rumors about her.)
- **If Randy loves Tressa, what will he do?** (Stop pressuring her—love always protects; respect her wishes instead of his desires—love is not self-seeking.)
- **What's the difference between infatuation and love?** (Infatuation is shallow, but love is deep; infatuation is selfish, love is unselfish.)

Say: **When we have a crush on someone, we usually think that person is perfect—physically, mentally, or even spiritually. But eventually we find out the person is human and flawed. Then *crash!*—the crush is over.**

Only God is perfect. No human is ever going to live up to all our expectations. But if we set realistic expectations for those we date, it will help us form healthy—and much less painful—relationships.

COMMITMENT
(5 to 10 minutes)

WANTED—THE IDEAL DATE

Give each person a sheet of paper and a marker. Ask kids each to make a "Wanted" poster listing five *realistic* qualities they'll look for in people they want to date. For example, kids might write "a Christian," "a sense of humor" or "sensitive." When kids are finished, have volunteers explain their posters.

Then form two groups—one for the guys and one for the girls—and have groups each form a circle. Have group members each tell one quality the person to their right has that would make that person "Wanted" for a relationship with a member of the opposite sex. It may be a quality from the posters or another positive quality.

When groups are finished, say: **Crushes come and go, but the qualities that allow for a lasting love relationship are alive in each of you. It's okay to enjoy the immediate fun of crushes, but remember that crushes can never match the lasting joy of true love.**

Table Talk

The Table Talk activity in this course helps junior highers, middle schoolers and their parents discuss sex, love and infatuation.

If you choose to use the Table Talk activity, this is a good time to show students the "Table Talk" handout (p. 19). Ask them to spend time with their parents completing it.

Before kids leave, give them each a photocopy of the "Table Talk" handout to take home, or tell them you'll be sending it to their parents. Tell kids to be prepared to report on their experiences with the handout next week.

Or use the Table Talk idea found in the Bonus Ideas (p. 43) for a meeting based on the handout.

CLOSING
(up to 5 minutes)

☐ OPTION 1: CRUSH

Pass out cans or bottles of Crush soft drinks.

Say: **We have seen that a crush is temporary, while love never ends. When we drink this "Crush" it will be gone, but each of you is worthy of love and has the ability to love.**

Drink a toast with the group to the joy of lasting love. After a few minutes, close with prayer, asking God to help kids be wise in choosing friends of the opposite sex, both now and in the future. Encourage kids to keep their cans or bottles of Crush as a reminder of the differences between infatuation and true love.

☐ OPTION 2: LOVE ME OR LEAVE ME

Have students stand in a circle and each complete the statement, "If someone didn't really love me but only had a crush on me, they would probably never realize that I am . . ."

The ending must be a positive characteristic.

After everyone has completed the statement, say: **Like I said before, crushes are fun, but love is worth waiting for. And each of you is worthy of love and has the ability to love.**

Close with prayer, thanking God that he loves us and asking him to guide kids in their future relationships.

If You Still Have Time . . .

Outrageous Flirts—Have students act out or describe the way they perceive members of the opposite sex flirting with them. Have kids tell what they think about people they see flirting.

I'm Crushed—Ask kids to share the kinds of things that make them stop having a crush on someone.

What You See . . .—Separate guys and girls into two groups and instruct them to decide the top five qualities they look for in members of the opposite sex.

Have volunteers from the girls' group act out through charades the top five qualities they look for in guys. Time the guys to see how fast they guess. Then switch and have the guys share their list through charades and time the girls' guesses. The team with the shortest overall time wins.

Cinderdude

Once you've received an assignment for a part, go into another room and run through the script with the other characters once or twice. Ham it up!

THE PLAYERS:

Narrator—reads the story and leaves a brief pause at each asterisk (*) for the players to act out what has just been read.

Cinderdude—the star of the show.

Horatio and Clementine—Cinderdude's lazy cousins.

Ms. Meany—the wicked aunt who takes care of Cinderdude.

Brilliant Belinda—the smart young woman who helps Cinderdude.

Ralph—the fairy god-dog.

THE STORY

Once upon a time there was a poor young man named Cinderdude (*), who was forced to live with his wicked aunt, Ms. Meany (*) and his lazy cousins, Horatio (*) and Clementine(*). They also had a dog named Ralph (*), who slept most of the time.

Every day Ms. Meany would sit in her chair reading magazines and eating candy bars (*). Horatio and Clementine played video games all day and fought over who won each game (*). This left Cinderdude to do all the work around the house.

Each morning he was forced to clean, clean, clean. He cleaned under the beds (*), over the cupboards (*), inside the toilets (*) and outside the dog house (*). It was dirty work, but Cinderdude was hardworking and cheerful.

One day a notice came in the mail that Brilliant Belinda, the smartest and prettiest girl in the land, was giving a party. Ms. Meany shoved Horatio and Clementine into her tiny car (*). Cinderdude tried to get in (*), but there was no room left (*).

Sadly, Cinderdude hung his head (*) and returned to the house. Suddenly he heard a voice. It was a deep, growling sort of voice that said, "Hey buddy, take the bus!"

Cinderdude looked around (*) and only saw Ralph. "Ralph? Did you say something?" he asked (*).

"Of course I did," Ralph growled (*). "I'm your fairy god-dog. Now if you'll just get up and take the bus to the party, I'm sure everything will work out fine." (*)

Cinderdude jumped up (*), patted Ralph on the head (*), and raced out to the bus stop (*).

At the party, Horatio and Clementine were busy playing video games and fighting (*). Ms. Meany was eating at the buffet (*). Cinderdude introduced himself to Brilliant Belinda and began telling her his life story (*). She was bored (*) so she gave him a book she had written on how to start your own business.

Cinderdude read the book (*), decided to start his own housecleaning business, and eventually became a millionaire. He bought a big house for himself and Ralph to live in, invited Beautiful Belinda to dinner (*), and lived happily ever after.

THE END

Table Talk

To the Parent: We're involved in a junior high course at church called *Love or Infatuation?* Students are exploring a Christian perspective on what love is and what it is not. They are deciding what is best in relationships with the opposite sex. We'd like you and your teenager to spend some time discussing this important topic. Use this "Table Talk" page to help you do that.

Parent

Pull out an old photo album or scrapbook. Show off some pictures of your early boyfriends or girlfriends. Tell your junior higher about your first crush.

- How did it start?
- Why did it end?
- Was there a time you had to break off a relationship? Why?
- How did you handle your feelings?

Junior higher

Discuss your responses to these open-ended statements with your parents.

- I hope to find a boyfriend or girlfriend who . . .
- The difference between being in love and having a crush is . . .
- I think the scariest thing about breaking up is . . .

Parent and junior higher

Complete these statements together.

- In relationships, communication is important because . . .
- Having sex outside of marriage is wrong because . . .
- I hope you will treat your future boyfriends or girlfriends . . .

Write five things you think are most important in a relationship with the opposite sex. Then tell why you chose these things:

Teenager	**Parent**
1.	1.
2.	2.
3.	3.
4.	4.
5.	5.

Read 1 Timothy 4:12. This verse says that even young people can be an example.

- How can someone set an example through love?
- What does God want our relationships to be examples of?
- How can we honor God even when a relationship is over?

LESSON 2

SEX IS NOT LOVE

Only a few decades ago, Lucy and Ricky Ricardo couldn't be shown sleeping in the same bed on television. But today's teenagers are bombarded with sexual images in movies, television, music and advertising. Unfortunately, these images often equate sex with love, leading kids to believe that love is little more than a biological function.

By helping kids see the difference between love and sex, we can help them make better choices in their relationships.

Note: During this lesson be sensitive to the fact that some members of your group may have already become sexually active. Like David and Bathsheba, we have to bear the consequences of our actions, but God still forgives us. Convey God's heart of forgiveness and reassure students that they *can* start fresh and treat themselves and their bodies with the respect God intended.

LESSON AIM

To help junior highers examine how sex should fit into the overall scheme of relationships.

OBJECTIVES

Students will:

- **discover how love and sexuality compare to a flower;**
- **examine the relationships of two biblical couples;**
- **commit to keeping themselves sexually pure; and**
- **tell lovable qualities they see in each other.**

BIBLE BASIS

RUTH 2:8-9, 13-16
2 SAMUEL 11:2-5

Look up the following scriptures. Then read the background paragraphs to see how the passages relate to your junior highers and middle schoolers.

Ruth 2:8-9, 13-16 tells of the kindness and thoughtfulness of Boaz toward Ruth.

As a young widow, Ruth followed harvesters in Boaz's fields, gathering grain for food. He befriended her, treated her with respect and even made sure she got special treatment.

In this story, kids can see the beginning of a romance that is based on love and respect. Boaz could have taken advantage of Ruth, but he looked out for her best interests instead. Their relationship is an example of godly love.

In **2 Samuel 11:2-5**, kids read of David's lust for the beautiful Bathsheba, their sexual relationships and her resulting pregnancy.

David was king and already had several wives. Even though David knew Bathsheba was married to one of his soldiers who was away at war, he gave in to temptation and had sex with her.

David's desire for Bathsheba was purely physical. Students can see that he was not looking out for her best interests or even his own. David allowed his desires to control him and disaster resulted. His example shows how real love does *not* act.

THIS LESSON AT A GLANCE

Section	Minutes	What Students Will Do	Supplies
Opener (Option 1)	5 to 10	**Don't Capture My Flag**—Try to take paper off each others' backs without having your own paper taken.	Paper, tape
(Option 2)		**Body-Parts Blizzard**—Match different body parts with a partner.	
Action and Reflection	10 to 15	**This Bud Is You**—Compare a new and "used" flower to their sexuality.	Two identical flowers
Bible Application	10 to 15	**Do You Love Me?**—Complete handout that explores the nature of true love.	"Do You Love Me?" handouts (p. 26), pencils, Bibles
Commitment	5 to 10	**Posies and Promises**—Commit to keeping themselves like new flowers.	Fresh flowers
Closing (Option 1)	up to 5	**Love Is . . .**—Exchange flowers and tell qualities of love they see in each other.	Flowers from Posies and Promises activity
(Option 2)		**The Couple to Copy**—Tell characteristics of Ruth or Boaz they see in each other.	

The Lesson

OPENER
(5 to 10 minutes)

☐ OPTION 1: DON'T CAPTURE MY FLAG

Tape a "flag" (a sheet of paper) on the back of each student. When you give the starting signal, have kids try to take the paper off of each other's backs, without having their own papers stolen. After a few minutes, call time and see if anyone's flag remains intact. Congratulate kids with flags intact as the winners.

After the game ask:

● **What was fun about this game?** (Trying to steal the flags; keeping others from taking my flag.)

● **How is trying to steal the flag off the others while protecting your own like "looking out for #1"?** (I wanted to be the only one left with a flag; I didn't care if others didn't want their flag taken.)

Say: **In this game you were looking out for what was best for you, even if it wasn't the best thing for someone else. Today we're going to see how choosing what is best for ourselves and others relates to love and sex.**

☐ OPTION 2: BODY-PARTS BLIZZARD

Form pairs and have partners go to opposite sides of the room and face the wall. As you read off a body-part combination, have kids each run to their partner, connect those body parts and freeze. For example, if you say "foot to head," one partner must put his or her foot on the other's head, then freeze in that position.

The last pair to freeze in position gets 10 points against them. Have kids return to their places on opposite sides of the room after each round. The pair with the lowest score at the end wins.

Use these combinations or others you think of yourself:

Ear to hand	Knee to elbow	Shin to chin
Nose to armpit	Heel to ear	Ankle to elbow
Hand to mouth	Nose to nose	Ear to knee

After the game, applaud the winners and ask:

● **How did you feel about this game?** (It was goofy; it felt uncomfortable.)

● **How are the uncomfortable positions you got into similar to relationships between girls and guys?** (Relationships often put you in uncomfortable positions; you don't always know who should take the lead in a relationship.)

Say: **Just like many relationships, some of you had to get into situations that were difficult or uncomfortable. But you chose to do it because you wanted to help your**

team win. This lesson will focus on choosing what is best for us when it comes to love and sex, so we can all come out winners.

Table Talk Follow-Up

If you sent the "Table Talk" handout (p. 19) to parents last week, discuss students' reactions to the activity. Ask volunteers to share what they learned from the discussion with their parents.

ACTION AND REFLECTION
(10 to 15 minutes)

THIS BUD IS YOU

Take two identical flowers and show them to the group.

Say: **I want everyone to see how beautiful these flowers are.**

Keep one flower for yourself and pass the other around and have each student touch it, smell it, even pull a petal or two from it. Pass it until it looks a little bruised or crumpled. Take the flower back from the students and hold it beside the fresh one.

Ask kids which flower they would rather have. Ask:

- **How did you feel as you saw the flower we passed becoming more and more bruised and torn?** (Sorry to see it ruined; I didn't understand why we were doing it.)
- **How is our sexuality like these flowers?** (We damage it by messing with it too much; it's fragile.)
- **If we loved this flower, what would we have done with it?** (Protected it; we wouldn't have passed it around.)
- **Flowers are beautiful and meant to be admired and smelled. But we admired this flower so roughly it ended up hurt. How is the way we treated this flower like having sex with someone you are not married to?** (It ruins the beauty of it; it's not right.)

Say: **A lot of people think of love and sex as being the same thing. But you can have sex with someone and never love them, and you can love someone and never have sex with them. Let's look at some people in the Bible who can help us see how love and sex are different.**

BIBLE APPLICATION
(10 to 15 minutes)

DO YOU LOVE ME?

Give kids each a Bible, a copy of the "Do You Love Me?" handout (p. 26) and a pencil. Have them work in groups of three or four to complete the handout.

When groups are finished, gather students together and ask:

- **Which of these couples treated each other like special flowers? Explain.** (Ruth and Boaz, they showed respect for each other.)

Read aloud Hebrews 13:4 and ask kids to comment on its

meaning. Then say: **Sex is a way to show love, but God has made it clear that it is an expression of love between married people.**

Ask:

● **Boaz made it clear to Ruth that he cared about her without even touching her. What are some ways we can show our love to boyfriends or girlfriends without getting physical?** (Writing notes; doing special things for the other person.)

● **What if your relationship is already really physical? What can you do to start relating in a way that God would approve?** (Don't spend time together late at night; start showing love in other ways.)

Say: **It's never too late to ask God's forgiveness for the way we've acted with a boyfriend or girlfriend in the past. And it's never too early to commit to keeping those relationships pure in the future.**

COMMITMENT
(5 to 10 minutes)

POSIES AND PROMISES

Ask:

● **If you were a flower right now, explain what kind you'd be and what condition you would be in.** (I'd be a dandelion because no one wants me around; I'd be a tulip bulb because I like to hide most of the time.)

● **What kind of flower do you think God wants you to be?** (Pure and perfect; beautiful and uncrumpled.)

● **Considering the kind of flower you think you are, is it possible to become the flower God intended? Why or why not?** (Yes, God will forgive me whatever I've done; no, sometimes the damage is too big to fix.)

Say: **No matter how much your flower has been hurt or crumpled through relationships, God has the power to give you a fresh start in love and in your sexuality.**

Give each person a fresh flower. Say: **This flower represents you. No matter what we've done in the past, we can start fresh. The more the flower gets passed, the more it gets bruised. Decide now to show yourself love by keeping yourself fresh and new as this flower.**

Have kids pray silently for a moment, asking God to fix their crumpled flowers and protect their sexuality in the future.

CLOSING
(up to 5 minutes)

☐ OPTION 1: LOVE IS . . .

Say: **Now that we've asked God to fix us, in his eyes we are all beautiful flowers, worthy of his unfailing love.**

Have kids go around the room and talk to three other people, each time telling the other person one quality that makes him or her worthy to be loved. For example, someone might say, "Your patience makes you worthy of love" or "Your kindness toward others makes you worthy to be loved." Make sure everyone feels included in the exchange.

When kids are finished, say: **God loves each of us and wants us to treat ourselves and each other with true love.**

☐ OPTION 2: THE COUPLE TO COPY

Say: **Now that we've asked God to fix us, in his eyes we are all beautiful flowers, capable of giving and receiving pure love from him and others.**

Have kids each find a partner, then tell one characteristic of Ruth or Boaz that they see in their partner's life. Close by having partners pray for each other, asking God to protect their sexuality and help them show true love.

If You Still Have Time . . .

Top 10 Reasons to Wait—Brainstorm a Top 10 list of reasons to wait until marriage to have sex.

Saying No—Read the following come-ons that students might hear from future dates. Have them think of quick replies to tell the person no.

1. If you loved me, you would sleep with me.
2. Everybody's doing it.
3. I'd do it for you.
4. We're going to get married anyway.
5. I want to show you how much I love you.

Kids may know of more come-ons that they can share with the group.

Do You Love Me?

Read Ruth 2:8-9, 13-16 and 2 Samuel 11:2-5. Explain to each other in your own words, what happened in each story.

After each of the following statements indicate whether you agree or disagree, and explain your answer to your partners.

	Agree	Disagree
1. Boaz treated Ruth with respect.	____	____
2. David treated Bathsheba with respect.	____	____
3. David had sex with Bathsheba to prove that he loved her.	____	____
4. Boaz loved Ruth.	____	____
5. Boaz was looking out for himself by helping Ruth.	____	____
6. David was concerned about what was best for Bathsheba.	____	____
7. It was Bathsheba's fault that David wanted to have sex with her.	____	____
8. Bathsheba could have told David no.	____	____

Discuss these questions with your partners:

- What is the difference between the way Boaz and Ruth acted and the way David and Bathsheba acted? Read 2 Samuel 11:6-17.
- Do you think having sex with Bathsheba was worth all the trouble it caused David? Why or why not?
- If you could write a letter to Bathsheba or David that they would read before they met each other, what would you say?

FRIENDS FIRST

LESSON 3

Junior high students will often choose a boyfriend or girlfriend on the basis of a few exchanged notes and the proddings of their friends. Some may actually go on a date. Then for some unknown reason, things just don't work out. Why?

Friendship is the basis of all healthy relationships. We can help students see how important friendship is and teach them to cultivate friendship in their dating lives.

LESSON AIM

To help junior highers discover that friendship is the foundation of all healthy relationships.

OBJECTIVES

Students will:

- **try to explain a seemingly common activity to a "time traveler";**
- **survey group members to learn more about the interests of others;**
- **commit to building friendships with members of the opposite sex; and**
- **tell about friendship-building qualities they see in each other.**

BIBLE BASIS

PHILIPPIANS 2:3-8

Look up the following scripture. Then read the background paragraphs to see how the passages relate to your junior highers and middle schoolers.

In **Philippians 2:3-8**, Paul writes about imitating Christ's humility in our relationships.

Selfishness often becomes a barrier to closeness with others. Paul explains here that we should consider others better than ourselves and be more concerned with their interests than our own.

All of us find it hard at times to put our own desires aside. Students will find that expressing genuine interest in what is important to others can improve their relationships with friends of both genders.

THIS LESSON AT A GLANCE

Section	Minutes	What Students Will Do	Supplies
Opener (Option 1)	5 to 10	**Three-Legged Race**—Race without talking with partners.	Strips of cloth or rope
(Option 2)		**Ring-Toss Relay**—"Ring" a member of the opposite sex in a relay.	Two hula hoops
Action and Reflection	15 to 20	**Time-Travel Troubles**—Explain simple activities to a cave person.	Paper, a pencil
Bible Application	10 to 15	**Interest Survey**—Survey group members' likes and dislikes.	"Interest Survey" handouts (p. 33), pencils
Commitment	5 to 10	**Balloon Brainstorm**—Name specific ways to build friendships with guys or girls.	Balloon, marker
Closing (Option 1)	up to 5	**Friendship Fan**—Make a fan filled with kids' positive comments.	Paper, pencils
(Option 2)		**My Treat**—Exchange candy as a symbol of friendship.	Candy

The Lesson

OPENER
(5 to 10 minutes)

☐ OPTION 1: THREE-LEGGED RACE

Tell the group that this game requires absolute silence. Have kids each become partners with a person sitting beside them. Pass out strips of cloth or rope to each couple and have them tie two of their legs together—without talking.

Have pairs each move to a starting line at one end of the room, then conduct a quick three-legged race. Tell kids that anyone who talks will be disqualified. Congratulate the winning couple, then ask:

- **What was difficult about this game?** (We couldn't talk about what we were going to do; it felt weird not to communicate.)
- **How would your chances of winning have been better if you could have talked with your partner?** (We could have developed a strategy; I could have encouraged my partner to run faster.)

Say: **Today we will see how it is hard to win at anything, whether it's a game or real life, without being able to communicate as friends.**

OPTION 2: RING-TOSS RELAY

Divide guys and girls. It's okay if teams are uneven. Ask for one volunteer from each group, then have the teams stand as indicated in the diagram in the margin.

guys lined up here	● girl volunteer
girls lined up here	● guy volunteer

Give the first person in each line a hula hoop. When you start the game, have the first person try to throw the hula hoop around the volunteer of the opposite sex, like a giant ring-toss game. After the first person throws the hoop, have the next person in line retrieve the hoop, return to the line, and try to make a "ringer." Continue until everyone has at least one turn. Encourage kids to toss the hoops gently. Teams get a point for each ringer they get. The people being ringed should remove glasses (if any) and protect themselves from being hit in the head, but they may not move to make being hooped more difficult.

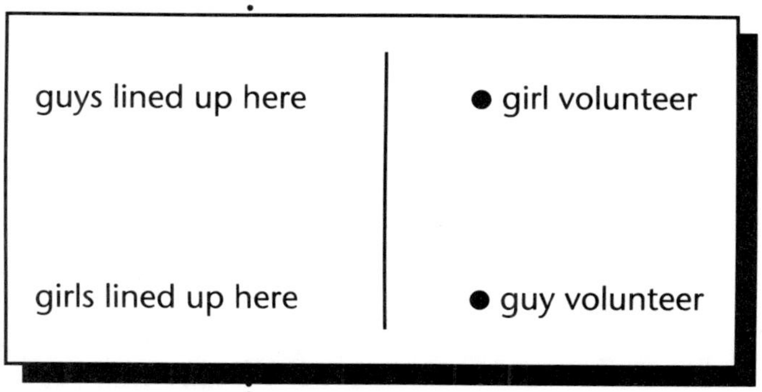

When you decide time is up, count the number of ringers and announce the winner.

Ask:

- **Did you like this game? Why or why not?** (Yes, it was fun; no, it was boring.)
- **How is this game like dating?** (It can be like a game; a lot of guys like to go after the same girl.)

Say: **In this game you tried to "ring" or catch a member of the opposite sex. Sometimes we have "ring-toss" relationships in real life. It's almost like we are trying to catch a boyfriend or girlfriend, without thinking about who that person really is on the inside. Today we are going to learn about the importance of being friends with members of the opposite sex.**

ACTION AND REFLECTION

(15 to 20 minutes)

TIME-TRAVEL TROUBLES

Form pairs. Give each pair a sheet of paper that has a different activity written on it. Here are several ideas for activities:

- starting a car,
- plugging in and turning on a light,
- making a phone call,
- typing the alphabet on a typewriter,
- making a glass of lemonade with ice in it and
- riding a bicycle.

Explain that you are a cave person who has just been transported from millions of years ago to the present through a strange accident. Say: **In order to get by, I'm going to have to learn how to do some things. Each pair has a paper with an activity on it. I need the partners to explain to me exactly how to do their activity.**

Give pairs each one or two minutes to explain their activity. Make the activity as difficult as possible for them to explain.

For example, if they say "Get in the car," ask "What's a car?" For every answer they give, ask another question.

After partners have made a brief attempt at their explanations, gather the students together. Ask:

• **How did you feel when you were trying to explain a simple activity to the cave person?** (Frustrated; I thought it was funny.)

• **How was this activity like trying to talk to a member of the opposite sex?** (Guys are cave men; girls ask too many questions; you can't figure out where they're coming from.)

• **What are some differences between the ways guys and girls communicate?** (Girls talk too much; guys brag a lot.)

Say: **Sometimes talking to members of the opposite sex is like talking to people from a different time. It seems like they don't understand us and we don't understand them. But if we don't communicate, things never work out and both sides become frustrated and confused. One way we can communicate better and build friendships with others is to learn more about them.**

BIBLE APPLICATION
(10 to 15 minutes)

INTEREST SURVEY

Hand out the "Interest Survey" handout (p. 33) and pencils. Give kids three minutes to fill out as much of the survey as possible. Encourage kids to get as many names as possible on their surveys.

After three minutes, gather the group together and see who was able to complete the survey. Ask:

• **Did you find out anything new about someone else in the group? What?**

Read aloud Philippians 2:3-8. Ask:

• **What do you think these verses mean?** (We should be interested in other people, not ourselves; we should put others first.)

• **How do you feel when people do know the things you are interested in, but they ignore those things?** (I feel left out; I feel like I'm not important to them.)

• **How do these verses apply to guy-girl relationships?** (You need to put the other person first; you have to genuinely care about the other person.)

• **How do you feel when someone you go out with agrees to do something you enjoy, though you know it's not his or her favorite activity?** (It makes me feel special; I believe they're really interested in me.)

Say: **When you were trying to communicate with the cave person, it was hard because you didn't have much in common. Now we have found a few things that we have in common, and we know it's important to put others' interests before our own. That's the basis for friendship.**

BALLOON BRAINSTORM

Inflate a balloon and write the word "friendship" on it. Have students sit in a circle and bounce the balloon around. Every few bounces, stop the play and have the person with the ball tell one *specific* thing he or she is is going to do to build friendships with members of the opposite sex. For example, "I'm going to listen when my boyfriend talks, instead of interrupting him all the time," or "I'm going to ask some girls what they think about things, instead of just talking about nothing."

After kids have each had a turn, remind them that they have made these commitments in public. Challenge them to live up to their statements and to hold each other accountable.

Say: **From our commitments today, it's easy to see that love and friendship can be expressed in lots of different ways. And each of us is uniquely gifted to express friendship and love to others—especially those of the opposite sex.**

COMMITMENT

(5 to 10 minutes)

☐ OPTION 1: FRIENDSHIP FAN

Form a circle. Say: **I'm going to pass a paper around the room. On this paper, write vertically, the name of the person on your left and the one friendship-building quality you admire in that person. Such as "a caring attitude," "interest in other people," or "enthusiasm." Then fold that section of the paper to begin making a fan. We'll continue around the circle at least once until our fan is completed.**

See the diagram in the margin for an example of this activity. When the paper is filled, complete the folding of the fan as illustrated in the diagram.

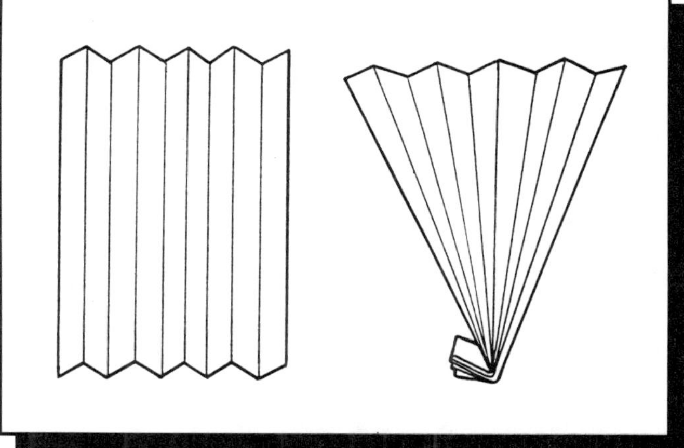

Say: **Friendship is like a fan on a hot day. It can cool off the hot spots that sometimes occur between girls and guys. I'll pass this fan around again for you to read about each person's friendship qualities. We'll keep the fan in our room as encouragement to always build friendships with those you want to date.**

CLOSING

(up to 5 minutes)

☐ OPTION 2: MY TREAT

Give each person a piece of candy. Tell the students that they must each give the treat to another person in the group and tell that person one way his or her friendship is a treat to others. For example, someone might say, "Your friendship is a treat because you're so giving" or "Your friendship is a treat because you're so funny." Kids may only receive one piece of candy to ensure that everyone is included.

When kids are finished, say: **Take your treats home as an**

encouragement to always remember to "treat" yourself right by building friendships first.

If You Still Have Time . . .

Create a Date—In groups of three or four, have kids come up with the best and most creative group date that costs less than $5 per person. Dates must promote communication and respect. When groups are ready, have the entire group vote on the best date.

To Make Me Feel Special—Have kids tell something that a member of the opposite sex could do to make them feel special.

Interest Survey

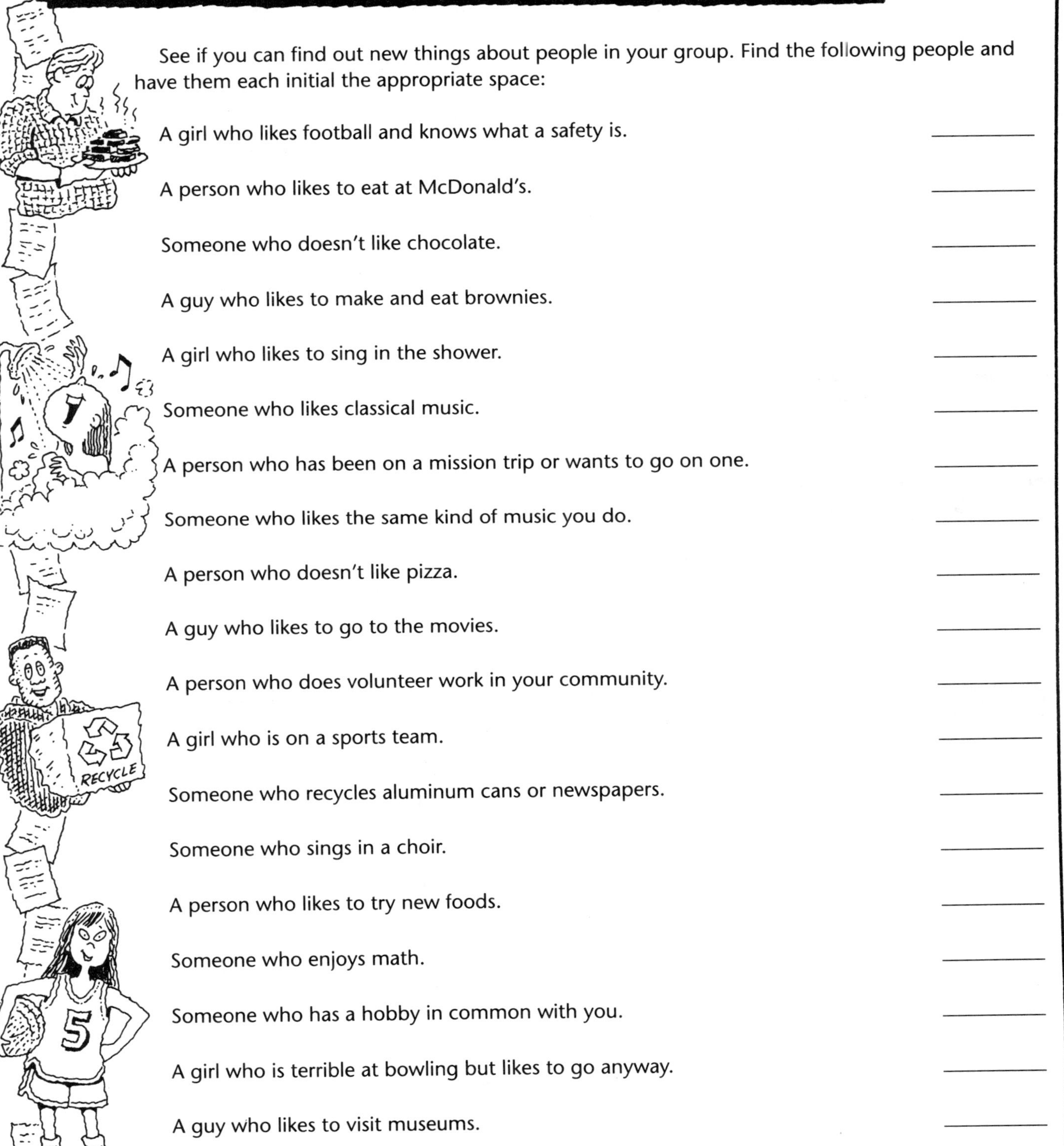

See if you can find out new things about people in your group. Find the following people and have them each initial the appropriate space:

A girl who likes football and knows what a safety is. __________

A person who likes to eat at McDonald's. __________

Someone who doesn't like chocolate. __________

A guy who likes to make and eat brownies. __________

A girl who likes to sing in the shower. __________

Someone who likes classical music. __________

A person who has been on a mission trip or wants to go on one. __________

Someone who likes the same kind of music you do. __________

A person who doesn't like pizza. __________

A guy who likes to go to the movies. __________

A person who does volunteer work in your community. __________

A girl who is on a sports team. __________

Someone who recycles aluminum cans or newspapers. __________

Someone who sings in a choir. __________

A person who likes to try new foods. __________

Someone who enjoys math. __________

Someone who has a hobby in common with you. __________

A girl who is terrible at bowling but likes to go anyway. __________

A guy who likes to visit museums. __________

LESSON 4

BREAKING AWAY

Many junior highers go steady and break up at about the same rate they change clothes. But these breakups often leave behind hurt feelings and hardness toward members of the opposite sex.

We can help kids see that ending a relationship doesn't mean the end of the world. In fact, it can be a new beginning.

LESSON AIM

To help junior highers learn how to handle relationships when they end.

OBJECTIVES

Students will:

- **break up with group members in various ways;**
- **act out positive and negative ways of ending a dating relationship;**
- **write a "Dear John" letter to themselves; and**
- **see the fragility of their own hearts.**

BIBLE BASIS

LUKE 6:27-28, 31
GALATIANS 5:15

Look up the following scriptures. Then read the background paragraphs to see how the passages relate to your junior highers and middle schoolers.

In **Luke 6:27-28, 31**, Jesus tells us how to treat those who are against us.

In this passage, Jesus gives specific instructions to those who are mistreated. Instead of fighting back, we are to show love to our enemies. This section concludes with the golden rule, which commands us to treat others as we want to be treated.

From Jesus' words, kids will see that there are positive ways to end relationships—ways that bring about good instead of harm.

In **Galatians 5:15**, Paul warns of the results of constant bickering and fighting.

God wants his people to love each other and to be examples of love to others. When anger and hatred come between us, love is destroyed. By seeing their situation from God's perspective, junior highers can see how bitter feelings can hurt them as well as others.

THIS LESSON AT A GLANCE

Section	Minutes	What Students Will Do	Supplies
Opener (Option 1)	5 to 10	**Bombs Away!**—Bomb each other with newspapers.	Old newspapers
(Option 2)		**Heartbreakers**—Break the balloon "hearts" of other teams while protecting their own.	Balloons
Action and Reflection	15 to 20	**Break It Up**—Experience breaking off from a group.	"Instruction Sheet A" handouts (p. 40), "Instruction Sheet B" handouts (p. 41), scissors
Bible Application	10 to 15	**A Date With the Bible**—Create and perform skits illustrating biblical relationships.	Bibles
Commitment	5 to 10	**Dear John . . .**—Write a letter breaking up with themselves.	"Dear John . . ." handouts (p. 42), pencils
Closing (Option 1)	up to 5	**Toilet-Paper Tie-Up**—Tie and untie strips of toilet paper.	Toilet paper
(Option 2)		**Balloon Hearts**—Draw their hearts on a balloon.	Balloons, straight pin, markers

The Lesson

OPENER
(5 to 10 minutes)

☐ OPTION 1: BOMBS AWAY!

Form two teams. Have teams go to opposite sides of the room and indicate a dividing line between them. Give each team a stack of old newspapers. Allow teams one minute to make "bombs" by crumpling the paper into balls.

On "go," have teams bomb opposing team members. When someone is hit with a paper ball, they "die" and must stop throwing balls immediately and lie down. The team with the last person left standing wins.

Ask:

- **How is this little war like what happens when guys and girls break up? How is it different? Explain.** (They try to throw a lot of stuff at each other; nobody really got hurt here, but people do get hurt in breakups.)

Say: **In this war we threw paper bombs at each other.**

But when we break up with someone, we often throw other kinds of bombs and end up with a lot of wounded feelings. Today, we'll talk about how we can avoid being wounded and wounding others in relationships.

☐ OPTION 2: HEARTBREAKERS

Form teams of three or four. Give each team a balloon to blow up. This balloon is the "heart" of the team. When it is broken, that team can no longer play.

On "go," have teams each try to break the balloons of other teams while protecting their own balloon. The last team with an unpopped balloon wins.

After the game, say: **Some teams were better at protecting their "hearts" than others. And some teams were better at breaking hearts than others. In real life, it's easy to have our hearts broken and to break other's hearts. Today we'll try to find ways of ending relationships without leaving a bunch of broken hearts lying around.**

ACTION AND REFLECTION

(15 to 20 minutes)

BREAK IT UP

Photocopy the "Instruction Sheet A" handout (p. 40) and cut each sheet of paper into four pieces. Make enough so that each student can have one set of instructions. Fold each piece in half so that students cannot see what is written on others' papers.

Also make photocopies of the "Instruction Sheet B" handout (p. 41) and cut them into four pieces. Fold these so they look like the others, but keep track of which are the breakup instructions.

Form groups of four.

Say: **I would like each group to find as many reasons as possible why a guy and girl who like each other should not go steady. But before you begin, I have a piece of paper for each of you. Please keep it folded until I tell you to look at it.**

Hand out the folded papers to students being sure that one person in each group has one of the "Instruction Sheet B" papers. Remind kids not to look at each other's papers. Don't let students know that some papers are different from others.

Have groups begin their discussion. After one or two minutes, instruct kids to read their papers without letting others see what is written. Then have them continue their discussion.

Give the groups enough time for the dissenter to try to leave the group. Then gather all of the groups together.

Ask:

- **What happened in your groups?** (We couldn't keep our group together; we ended up fighting.)
- **How did you feel when one of your group members tried to leave? Explain.** Confused because I didn't know why he wanted to leave; mad because she was rude and I was

trying to keep the group together.)

● **How was the person in your group leaving the activity like breaking up with a boyfriend or girlfriend?** (Feelings get hurt; you feel helpless when the other person wants to break up and you don't.)

● **When is breaking up with a boyfriend or girlfriend the best thing?** (If she is a bad influence; if he pressures you to have sex.)

● **Even if you know breaking up is the best thing, how does it make you feel?** (Like a failure; like no one will ever love me.)

Say: **It may be your choice to end a relationship, or it may be the other person's choice. Either way, you can make breaking up easier—or harder. Let's learn more about different ways to end a relationship.**

BIBLE APPLICATION

(10 to 15 minutes)

A DATE WITH THE BIBLE

Form two groups. Have one group read Luke 6:27-28, 31 and the other read Galatians 5:15. Ask groups each to create and perform a short skit that illustrates their scripture passage in relation to ending a dating relationship. Tell kids that the only rule is that everyone must be involved in the acting—either as an actor or as a prop.

Give groups a few minutes to prepare, then have them each perform their skit. After the skits, read both scripture passages aloud to the entire group.

Ask:

● **If someone is "biting and devouring" when a relationship ends, what does that mean?** (Gossiping about the other person; saying rude things.)

● **How does that make you feel?** (Like being mean back to them; like crawling into a hole.)

● **Even if someone is mean to you when they break up with you, what does the Bible say we should do?** (Pray for them; show love to them.)

● **How can we show love to those who hurt us?** (By not hurting them back; by treating them with respect.)

Say: **It's really hard to be loving to those who hurt us. It's a lot easier to be hateful and bitter. But that bitterness stays with us a long time and becomes a part of the way we act and treat others. Pretty soon we find out that we haven't just hurt others, but—like it says in Galatians 5:15—we have destroyed ourselves as well.**

COMMITMENT

(5 to 10 minutes)

DEAR JOHN . . .

Give each student a photocopy of the "Dear John . . ." handout (p. 42) and a pencil. Have students fill out the sheet and tell them to keep in mind the verses they read earlier.

When kids are finished, form pairs. Have partners discuss what they wrote on their handouts. Then have volunteers share with the entire group their partners' ideas.

Then form a circle and ask:

- **Was it hard to be positive writing this letter? Why or why not?** (Yes, because it's easier to hurt someone's feelings; no, because I was thinking about how I would want to be treated.)
- **How will you change the way you'll treat others when you want to end a relationship?** (I'll try to treat them with respect; I won't talk behind their backs.)

Say: **I hope none of you will have to break up with a friend any time soon. But eventually, everyone here will have to end a relationship. Let's try to remember how we would feel if we were in the other person's shoes and commit to treating them as we want to be treated.**

CLOSING
(up to 5 minutes)

☐ OPTION 1: TOILET-PAPER TIE-UP

Hand out two strips of toilet paper to each student. Have kids each tie their strips into the best knot they can without tearing either piece. When everyone has tied their knots, have them *untie* the knots without breaking or tearing either piece. If anyone is able to do this, congratulate them.

Ask: **How is untying this knot like trying to break up with a boyfriend or girlfriend?** (We get hurt easily; you have to be really careful.)

Say: **These pieces of toilet paper are fragile and are ruined easily. We are like that too. Our feelings are easily hurt. Whether we are in a relationship, or trying to "untie" a relationship, we need to treat each other with an awareness of how fragile our hearts really are.**

Have kids each pray aloud for the person on their right, thanking God for one gentle, loving quality that person demonstrates in relating to others.

☐ OPTION 2: BALLOON HEARTS

Give kids each a balloon and a marker. Have kids each inflate their balloon and draw a large heart on it. On the other side of the balloon, have kids each write their name.

Hold up a straight pin and say: **Our hearts are a lot like these balloons. All it takes is one sharp jab from someone close to us, and our hearts will break.**

Pretend to jab at a few balloons, but then stop and say: **Take your balloons home as a reminder of how fragile our hearts are. If we live with that in mind, breakups might not leave our hearts shattered on the floor.**

Have kids each pray aloud for the person on their right, thanking God for one gentle, loving quality that person demonstrates in relating to others.

If You Still Have Time . . .

Debate—Form two groups. Name one group "Yes" and the other "No." Read the following statements and give each group 30 seconds to defend their viewpoint, even if in real life they don't agree.

- You have been going out with the same person for a few weeks and then meet a new person you'd like to date. Should you go out with the new person?
- You really like someone who is not a Christian. Should you go out with that person?
- Your parents don't like your boyfriend or girlfriend because they think he or she is a bad influence on you. Should you break up?
- Your boyfriend or girlfriend keeps pressuring you to have sex. Should you break up?
- Should junior highers go steady?

Course Reflection—Form a circle. Ask students to reflect on the past four lessons. Have them take turns completing the following sentences:

- Something I learned from this course is . . .
- If I could tell my friends about this course, I'd say . . .
- Something I'll do differently because of this course is . . .

INSTRUCTION SHEET "A"

Photocopy and cut apart these instructions to use in the Action and Reflection section.

For this activity to work, it is **very** important that your group stay together. Try to be positive and keep your group working together.

For this activity to work, it is **very** important that your group stay together. Try to be positive and keep your group working together.

For this activity to work, it is **very** important that your group stay together. Try to be positive and keep your group working together.

For this activity to work, it is **very** important that your group stay together. Try to be positive and keep your group working together.

INSTRUCTION SHEET "B"

Photocopy and cut apart these instructions to use in the Action and Reflection section.

You're tired of being in this group. Come up with an excuse to leave the group and say that you are going to join another group.

Begin to argue with everyone and complain about the group. Tell the others you don't want to be in the group anymore and you don't see any reason to do this stupid activity.

Tell everyone that you don't think you want to be a part of the group any more. Be very polite and thank them for helping in the activity. Continue being polite, but insist on leaving the group.

Be rude to group members and complain that they never do things the way you want to. Tell them if they don't start using your answers then you are leaving. Leave even if they *do* use your answers.

Dear John
Pretend that your boyfriend or girlfriend is breaking up with you. They are going to write you a letter to end the relationship. Help them write this letter so that it won't hurt your feelings. Think about how you want to be treated.
Dear ______________________ (your name)
I am sorry to tell you this, but I want to break up with you because:
While we were going out I really appreciated these two things about you:
I hope that in the future:
Thank you for:
Let's try to remember all the good things about our relationship. I hope that we can still be friends.
Sincerely,

BONUS IDEAS

MEETINGS AND MORE

Bonus Scriptures—The lessons focus on a select few scripture passages, but if you'd like to incorporate more Bible readings into the lessons, here are our suggestions:

- Genesis 29:1-30 (Jacob falls in love with Rachel.)
- Proverbs 2:1-22 (Solomon warns his son to avoid the snare of the adulteress.)
- Proverbs 5:1-23 (Solomon advises his son to turn away from lust.)
- 1 Corinthians 7:25-38 (Paul discusses the advantages of celibacy.)
- Ephesians 5:22-33 (Paul compares a love relationship to the relationship between Christ and the church.)
- 2 Timothy 2:20-22 (Paul encourages Timothy to set himself apart as a person of honor.)

Ask the Experts—Invite doctors, nurses or other health professionals from your church or community to talk to students about sex, pregnancy and sexually transmitted diseases. Kids may feel more comfortable meeting with guys in one room and girls in another. Have students write questions anonymously and let your experts answer as many as time permits.

Parents may appreciate being notified of such a meeting and may want to attend.

Book Pass-Along—Get one or two copies of Ray Short's *Sex, Love or Infatuation* (Augsburg Fortress). Have a student check out the book and bring it back the next week for another student to check out. Plan a time to talk about their discoveries.

Famous Faces—Have kids bring their favorite magazines or posters of people of the opposite sex they really admire. Have kids discuss how these people are revered by fans and how that kind of "crush" is different than a true relationship. Have kids compare being a "fan" and being close to someone you really know.

Table Talk—Use the Table Talk handout (p. 19) as the basis for a meeting with parents and teenagers. During the meeting, have parents and kids complete the handout and discuss it.

- Ask parents to bring photos or other mementos from their early dating days to share with their kids.
- If you can talk any parents into modeling their old prom attire—or having their kids model it—you could put on a little night of nostalgia.

● Have a few of the parents share their funniest date, worst date or most embarrassing date. Kids won't believe their parents were ever in a situation they now face!

Group Date—Form groups of five or fewer and have groups each plan a "date" for the entire youth group. Groups must consider cost and time limitations. Have a phone, phone book and current newspaper available. Give groups each the opportunity to present their "date," vote on a winner and go!

Barbie and Ken Break Up—Have any interested students make a video or slide show using Barbie and Ken dolls, or any others that you may prefer. The title should be *The Breakup.* Let kids write their own script and make their own props. When the production is complete, show it to the entire group.

Panel Pals—Gather a group of singles of both genders from different age groups (the wider the range the better) and from different single statuses (never married, widowed, divorced). Allow students to question them about what they look for in new relationships, what they have learned from old ones, and how they have changed through their past relationships.

Pregnancy Center Visit—Take students to a crisis pregnancy center or have the director of a facility talk to your group. Students can learn that pregnancy really does result from sex and that it will change their lives, whether they are the mother or the father.

This may spark a discussion about abortions and options in pregnancy, so be prepared. Also, some parents may not want their child to participate in an event of this nature.

Date Rape Discussion—Read aloud one or two articles on date rape to students. Some good examples are: "Preventing Date Rape," by Dr. David Elkind in Parents, April 1989, page 198; and "Dating Violence: Troubled Love," by Whitney Woodward in 'Teen, April 1990, page 12. Either of these can be obtained at the public library. Your librarian can also help you find more articles.

Discuss reasons that date rape happens, why it is wrong, and what can be done by both guys and girls to prevent it.

Some of your students may have been raped or sexually abused. Be sensitive to their feelings and don't allow the conversation to bring blame to the victim.

Music Messages—Have kids each bring a recording of their favorite secular song to the meeting. Play some of the songs. After each song have students rate the song on the "Music Messages" handout (p. 46). After rating several songs have kids tell how the ratings surprised them, then discuss the questions on the handout.

PARTY PLEASER

Valentine's Costume Party—Even if February is long past, help your kids plan and throw a Valentine's Day party complete with pink, red and white decorations. Serve ice cream sundaes with cherry topping.

Have students come as famous duos or trios, such as the Three Musketeers, Laurel and Hardy, Fred and Wilma Flintstone, Homer and Marge Simpson. Or they can come as a single member of a couple, such as David without Goliath, or Little Red Riding Hood without the Big Bad Wolf.

RETREAT IDEA

Dating Game Retreat—Use the old *Dating Game* TV show as a basis for several retreat meetings on various topics related to dating. Topics could include choosing a date, asking someone out, things to do on a date or keeping hormones under control. Use the devotions on love and marriage from *The Youth Bible* (Word/Group) to discuss modern and biblical examples of love as references for appropriate attitudes and actions.

End the retreat with a *Dating Game* episode in which winners will receive an all-expenses-paid date (chaperoned by a youth leader).

To select contestants for this game, ask all who would like to be considered to write 10 questions to ask a potential date. Choose one guy and three girls for the first round, and one girl and three guys for the second round.

Chaperone the four winners on an inexpensive date as their prize. Take along a video camera to capture the evening's events for the rest of the group to see at your next meeting.

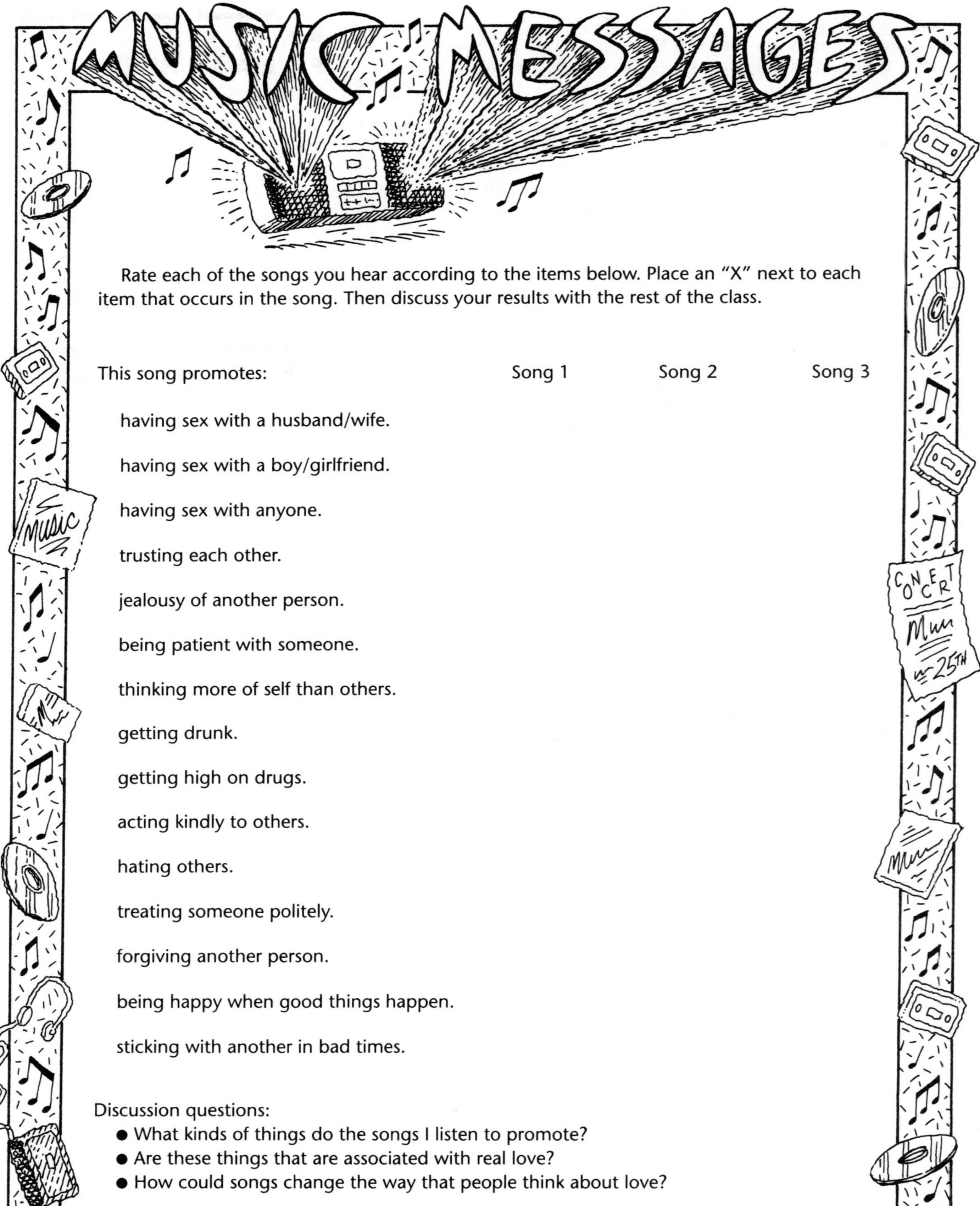

Rate each of the songs you hear according to the items below. Place an "X" next to each item that occurs in the song. Then discuss your results with the rest of the class.

This song promotes:	Song 1	Song 2	Song 3
having sex with a husband/wife.			
having sex with a boy/girlfriend.			
having sex with anyone.			
trusting each other.			
jealousy of another person.			
being patient with someone.			
thinking more of self than others.			
getting drunk.			
getting high on drugs.			
acting kindly to others.			
hating others.			
treating someone politely.			
forgiving another person.			
being happy when good things happen.			
sticking with another in bad times.			

Discussion questions:

- What kinds of things do the songs I listen to promote?
- Are these things that are associated with real love?
- How could songs change the way that people think about love?

CURRICULUM REORDER—TOP PRIORITY

Order now to prepare for your upcoming Sunday school classes, youth ministry meetings, and weekend retreats! Each book includes all teacher and student materials—plus photocopiable handouts—for any size class . . . for just $8.99 each!

FOR SENIOR HIGH:

1 & 2 Corinthians: Christian Discipleship, ISBN 1-55945-230-7

Angels, Demons, Miracles & Prayer, ISBN 1-55945-235-8

Changing the World, ISBN 1-55945-236-6

Christians in a Non-Christian World, ISBN 1-55945-224-2

Christlike Leadership, ISBN 1-55945-231-5

Communicating With Friends, ISBN 1-55945-228-5

Counterfeit Religions, ISBN 1-55945-207-2

Dating Decisions, ISBN 1-55945-215-3

Dealing With Life's Pressures, ISBN 1-55945-232-3

Deciphering Jesus' Parables, ISBN 1-55945-237-4

Exodus: Following God, ISBN 1-55945-226-9

Exploring Ethical Issues, ISBN 1-55945-225-0

Faith for Tough Times, ISBN 1-55945-216-1

Forgiveness, ISBN 1-55945-223-4

Getting Along With Parents, ISBN 1-55945-202-1

Getting Along With Your Family, ISBN 1-55945-233-1

The Gospel of John: Jesus' Teachings, ISBN 1-55945-208-0

Hazardous to Your Health: AIDS, Steroids & Eating Disorders, ISBN 1-55945-200-5

Is Marriage in Your Future?, ISBN 1-55945-203-X

Jesus' Death & Resurrection, ISBN 1-55945-211-0

The Joy of Serving, ISBN 1-55945-210-2

Knowing God's Will, ISBN 1-55945-205-6

Life After High School, ISBN 1-55945-220-X

Making Good Decisions, ISBN 1-55945-209-9

Money: A Christian Perspective, ISBN 1-55945-212-9

Movies, Music, TV & Me, ISBN 1-55945-213-7

Overcoming Insecurities, ISBN 1-55945-221-8

Psalms, ISBN 1-55945-234-X

Real People, Real Faith: Amy Grant, Joni Eareckson Tada, Dave Dravecky, Terry Anderson, ISBN 1-55945-238-2

Responding to Injustice, ISBN 1-55945-214-5

Revelation, ISBN 1-55945-229-3

School Struggles, ISBN 1-55945-201-3

Sex: A Christian Perspective, ISBN 1-55945-206-4

Today's Lessons From Yesterday's Prophets, ISBN 1-55945-227-7

Turning Depression Upside Down, ISBN 1-55945-135-1

What Is the Church?, ISBN 1-55945-222-6

Who Is God?, ISBN 1-55945-218-8

Who Is Jesus?, ISBN 1-55945-219-6

Who Is the Holy Spirit?, ISBN 1-55945-217-X

Your Life as a Disciple, ISBN 1-55945-204-8

FOR JUNIOR HIGH/MIDDLE SCHOOL:

Accepting Others: Beyond Barriers & Stereotypes, ISBN 1-55945-126-2

Advice to Young Christians: Exploring Paul's Letters, ISBN 1-55945-146-7

Applying the Bible to Life, ISBN 1-55945-116-5

Becoming Responsible, ISBN 1-55945-109-2

Bible Heroes: Joseph, Esther, Mary & Peter, ISBN 1-55945-137-8

Boosting Self-Esteem, ISBN 1-55945-100-9

Building Better Friendships, ISBN 1-55945-138-6

Can Christians Have Fun?, ISBN 1-55945-134-3

Caring for God's Creation, ISBN 1-55945-121-1

Christmas: A Fresh Look, ISBN 1-55945-124-6

Competition, ISBN 1-55945-133-5

Dealing With Death, ISBN 1-55945-112-2

Dealing With Disappointment, ISBN 1-55945-139-4

Doing Your Best, ISBN 1-55945-142-4

Drugs & Drinking, ISBN 1-55945-118-1

Evil and the Occult, ISBN 1-55945-102-5

Genesis: The Beginnings, ISBN 1-55945-111-4

Guys & Girls: Understanding Each Other, ISBN 1-55945-110-6

Handling Conflict, ISBN 1-55945-125-4

Heaven & Hell, ISBN 1-55945-131-9

Is God Unfair?, ISBN 1-55945-108-4

Love or Infatuation?, ISBN 1-55945-128-9

Making Parents Proud, ISBN 1-55945-107-6

Making the Most of School, ISBN 1-55945-113-0

Materialism, ISBN 1-55945-130-0

The Miracle of Easter, ISBN 1-55945-143-2

Miracles!, ISBN 1-55945-117-3

Peace & War, ISBN 1-55945-123-8

Peer Pressure, ISBN 1-55945-103-3

Prayer, ISBN 1-55945-104-1

Reaching Out to a Hurting World, ISBN 1-55945-140-8

Sermon on the Mount, ISBN 1-55945-129-7

Suicide: The Silent Epidemic, ISBN 1-55945-145-9

Telling Your Friends About Christ, ISBN 1-55945-114-9

The Ten Commandments, ISBN 1-55945-127-0

Today's Faith Heroes: Madeline Manning Mims, Michael W. Smith, Mother Teresa, Bruce Olson, ISBN 1-55945-141-6

Today's Media: Choosing Wisely, ISBN 1-55945-144-0

Today's Music: Good or Bad?, ISBN 1-55945-101-7

What Is God's Purpose for Me?, ISBN 1-55945-132-7

What's a Christian?, ISBN 1-55945-105-X

Order today from your local Christian bookstore, or write: Group Publishing, Box 485, Loveland, CO 80539. For mail orders, please add postage/handling of $4 for orders up to $15, $5 for orders of $15.01+. Colorado residents add 3% sales tax.

MORE PROGRAMMING IDEAS FOR YOUR ACTIVE GROUP...

DO IT! ACTIVE LEARNING IN YOUTH MINISTRY

Thom and Joani Schultz

Discover the keys to teaching creative faith-building lessons that teenagers look forward to...and remember for a lifetime. You'll learn how to design simple, fun programs that will help your kids...

- build community,
- develop communication skills,
- relate better to others,
- experience what it's really like to be a Christian,

...and apply the Bible to their daily challenges. Plus, you'll get 24 ready-to-use active-learning exercises complete with debriefing questions and Bible application. For example, your kids will...

- learn the importance of teamwork and the value of each team member by juggling six different objects as a group,
- experience community and God's grace using a doughnut,
- grow more sensitive to others' needs by acting out Matthew 25:31-46

...just to name a few. And the practical index of over 30 active-learning resources will make your planning easier.

ISBN 0-931529-94-8

DEVOTIONS FOR YOUTH GROUPS ON THE GO

Dan and Cindy Hansen

Now it's easy to turn every youth group trip into an opportunity for spiritual growth for your kids. This resource gives you 52 easy-to-prepare devotions that teach meaningful spiritual lessons using the experiences of your group's favorite outings. You'll get devotions perfect for everything from amusement parks, to choir trips, to miniature golf, to the zoo. Your kids will gain new insights from the Bible as they...

- discuss how many "strikes" God gives us—after enjoying a game of softball,
- experience the hardship of Jesus' temptation in the wilderness—on a camping trip,
- understand the disciples' relief when Jesus calmed the storm—while white-water rafting, even

...learn to trust God's will when bad weather cancels an event or the bus breaks down!

Plus, the handy topical listing makes your planning easy.

ISBN 1-55945-075-4